Proof Something Happened

Also by Tony Trigilio

Poetry

The Lama's English Lessons (2006)
Make a Joke and I Will Sigh and You Will Laugh and I Will Cry (2008)
With the Memory, Which is Enormous (2009)
Historic Diary (2011)
White Noise (2013)
The Complete *Dark Shadows* (of My Childhood), Book 1 (2014)
Inside the Walls of My Own House (2016)
Ghosts of the Upper Floor (2019)

Criticism

"Strange Prophecies Anew": Rereading Apocalypse in Blake, H.D, and Ginsberg
(2000)
Allen Ginsberg's Buddhist Poetics (2007)

Editor

Visions and Divisions: American Immigration Literature, 1870-1930 (with Tim
Prchal, 2008)
Elise Cowen: Poems and Fragments (2014)
Dispatches from the Body Politic: Interviews with Jan Beatty, Meg Day, and
Douglas Kearney (2016)

Proof Something Happened

☙

Tony Trigilio

Marsh Hawk Press • 2021
East Rockaway, New York

Marsh Hawk Press, Inc. is a not-for-profit corporation under
section 501(c)3 United States Internal Revenue Code.

Text: Palatino Linotype

Manufactured in the United States of America

11 12 13 7 6 5 4 3 2 1 First Edition

ISBN: 978-0-9969912-3-0

Marsh Hawk Press
P.O. Box 206, East Rockaway, N.Y. 11518-0206
mheditor@marshhawkpress.org

Acknowledgments

Thanks to the editors of the following journals and anthologies in which poems from this book originally appeared, often in different versions:

Big Other: "Missing Time"; "Transcript: Barney Hill's Hypnosis"; "Extraordinary claims require extraordinary evidence"; "Beeping sounds in isolated locations all over the world, driving away animals"; "If She Only Had Proof Something Happened"; "The two witnesses prophesied for 1,260 days wearing sackcloths"; "From Outer Space with Love"; and "Betty Hill, 'Sightings Journal': April 28, 1978."

Black Tongue Review: "He felt two fingers pulling back his mouth. The glow wasn't from an object in his hand" and "They were all dressed alike. Betty wasn't really prepared for their appearance."

Columbia Poetry Review: "Dr. Simon put Barney Hill under hypnosis. Barney described the humanoids. David Baker drew them"; "He was told not to open his eyes and it would be over quickly and he could be on his way"; "The Orb"; "Sightings Journal"; and "Oct. 23, 1975: Tom Snyder Interviews Betty Hill on *The Tomorrow Show.*"

Dispatches from the Poetry Wars: "He still believed what he was seeing had a rational explanation" and "Then she thought if they're so smart, let them find Barney's grave without her help."

The Eloquent Poem (Persea Books): *"The UFO Incident."*

Fifth Wednesday Journal: "'Over time other miracles occurred, but these were the most important ones.'" Winner of the 2016 *Fifth Wednesday* Editors' Prize in Poetry.

Ghost Town: "'What I'm saying is part of me outside the actual creation of words themselves'" and "She felt very stupid because she didn't know where earth was on the map."

Salt Hill: "'My soul sometimes floats out of my body. I don't listen to the radio while driving.'"

South Dakota Review: "'Now do you believe in flying saucers?'"

I am indebted to Susan Howe for selecting this manuscript, and to Marsh Hawk Press, especially Sandy McIntosh and Ed Foster. Thank you to Jan Bottiglieri, Kevin Cassell, Brian Cremins, Matthew DeMarco, Allison Felus, Chris Green, Larry Janowski, John Madera, Mark O'Connell, Liz Shulman, Michael Trigilio, David Trinidad, and Dominique Wagner. Gratitude to the staff of The Douglas and Helena Milne Special Collections and Archives Department at the University of New Hampshire, and to Mark Rodeghier, President and Scientific Director of the J. Allen Hynek Center for UFO Studies. This book was completed with the help of a Faculty Development Grant from Columbia College Chicago.

Contents

Introduction

This is a book of poems based on an historical incident. On September 19, 1961, Betty and Barney Hill were driving home to Portsmouth, New Hampshire, after a three-day vacation in Niagara Falls and Montreal. Around 10:30 that evening, near Lancaster, New Hampshire, in the White Mountains, they noticed a bright light in the sky that seemed to be following them. The light grew larger and brighter. Barney pulled the car over and stepped out to investigate with his binoculars. He observed a strange, disc-shaped aircraft, with approximately eleven crew members watching him through the craft's windows. He ran back to the car. The Hills drove away, but the aircraft continued to follow them. Their memories of the rest of the trip were fragmented and murky. They returned to Portsmouth safely, although they arrived seven hours after leaving Montreal in what should have been a four-hour drive. In 1964, during psychiatric sessions with Dr. Benjamin Simon, renowned for his use of hypnosis to treat combat-related stress disorders in World War II veterans, the Hills claimed to remember being captured by the crew members of the aircraft that had followed them that night in 1961. They recalled being taken from their car and brought inside the ship, after which the crew members allegedly performed invasive medical experiments on the couple before escorting them back to their car. Alien encounters had been reported in other parts of the world before, but because of the extensive detail documented in the Hills' experience, their story became one of the most famous cases of alleged alien abduction in U.S. history.

Every effort has been made in these poems to retain the language authentic to the time period (the mid- to late-twentieth century). Whether the book's language is adapted from actual archival documents or invented by the writer, its only purpose is to deepen the verisimilitude of the book's historical narrative.

Are we being robbed? They're men, all with black jackets, and I don't have any money. I don't have anything. They are standing in the road. They won't talk to me. Only the eyes are talking to me. I don't understand it. The eyes don't have a body. They're just eyes.

—Barney Hill

It's never off my mind. I had the feeling that if we had died they wouldn't have been too bothered.

—Betty Hill

Missing Time

Her turquoise ring vanished, pink mystery stains on her dress, silver-dollar
circles scorched on the Bel Air's trunk.

We can tell what happened but this doesn't mean we know more than when we
started.

If David Blaine, for instance, can turn a cup of steaming coffee into a handful of
coins, then it's crackpot *not* to believe in virgin birth or holy spirit.

It's terrifying to think through the body: if you touch the cup of coffee, it might
touch you back.

The ring turned up two weeks later under leaves inexplicably piled on the
kitchen counter.

Then she started to remember: *The drive should've taken four hours.*

"Now do you believe in flying saucers?"

How far from Concord? The radio
stopped working a long time ago.
How far from when they heard
the first beeps? Betty barely

remembered the roadside diner,
the hoodlum in slick black ducktail
eating a grapefruit at the counter
and keeping an eye on Barney.

A sack of bone-meal fertilizer steady
in the trunk. Staccato, stomp—
song of the blackout at daybreak—
electronic beeps like someone

dropped tuning forks all over
the back of the Bel Air. Staccato, fizz,
Betty sagged her cheek against
the passenger window, their car missing

in gimp thrusts, sputters. Stared
at the cigarette she didn't know
how to light. And Barney drowsy
at the wheel. She saw a man backlit

in the doorway of the AAA-approved
motel they passed as pencil lights
in the sky chased them round
every curve and bend, and they drove

and drove. Betty recalled the waitress
pouring coffee into a dirty cup
but didn't think she could ask
for a different one—it was that kind

of place: everyone looked at them
when they got out of their car
and here comes Barney who's black.

Later, revisiting the field, they learned

Barney walked so far he couldn't hear
Betty calling. Through binoculars,
the moon sat roly-poly on the ground
hours after it actually set. Why for two

weeks was Barney's neck so sore?
Why did his watch stop at 10:30?
If you can't believe it yourself
then you better not tell anyone,

especially with Barney's ulcers.
If something scares him, he pretends
it's not there. A half-dozen shapes,
at least, braced against those windows,

stared back as the silent pancake
tilted down at the two of them,
lit the dotted line in the middle
of the road.

"My soul sometimes floats out of my body. I don't listen to the radio while driving."

At least once in the past year, I've fallen asleep
then awakened the next morning in another room.

I was hunting for rabbits in Virginia, eight or nine

years old, and this cute little bunny fled into a bush,
my cousin Marge one side of the branches, and me

on the other—with a hat. About once each year,

I wake up during sleep unable to move. The creature
in the shiny black coat was looking at me, black scarf

draped around his neck and left shoulder. While sitting

quietly, I've had uplifting sensations as if driving over
a rolling road. At least once in my life very late

at night, I've felt the presence of another.

The poor bunny thought he was safe. I wanted to hear
a jet, kept thinking it was a plane—a cigar flying sideways

in front of the moon. Wanted to hear a hum.

To hear a motor. It's got to be—I'm a practiced
Piper Cub watcher and I wanted to hear a jet, badly.

It tickled me, the bunny just hiding behind a tiny stalk.

Bright moon, the dotted line between lanes, six beings
in black flagged me down. Next day, spots on the trunk

big as silver dollars made my compass needle spin.

They dragged me up a ramp and I didn't want to open
my eyes. I pounced, threw my hat on him and captured

the poor little rabbit who thought he was safe.

At least once a month I experience intense smells
that don't have an obvious source. I dream of floating

or flying through the air at least once per year.

A sky-blue hospital room—I'd stay there, pretend I'm
anywhere, think of God and Jesus and think I'm not

afraid. They dragged me up a ramp, laid me

on an operating table and put a cup over my groin.
Black Scarf said don't be afraid, I'd be safe.

I'm not a bunny. Not in the woods. Not on the road.

Anxious to get home and look at my groin.
If I made it back, I'd examine it, check to see

if it left a mark. Proof something happened to me.

"What I'm saying is part of me outside the actual creation of words themselves."

I sound like a song I can't remember. Some talk of how I broke the binocular strap that night. A pang in my rib, my ulcer. Too much to digest at one time, listening to that person playing himself. They made me forget what happened on that mountain road. Better to wonder than remember. Hearing my voice again, the soreness behind my head, parts of my life put back together like I was talking in my sleep. I tugged the strap, yanked the binoculars off my neck. Threw them in the back seat. My voice—I was lifted out of the driver's side. I didn't understand it was me. A wince in my rib. Dr. Simon hadn't heard this kind of terror in battlefield trauma cases he'd treated. Does this mean the sighting was real? Probably, he said, then backed off. Two of them looking down at my body, teardrop heads on bent stems. From the slit where a mouth would be, a hum for the life of me I can't find a name for. That person playing me can't see any windows—blue-sky fluorescent walls, examination room like a wedge cut from a pie. I am saying something about the ship choking us and the coarse sound when they scraped samples from my arm. They flew away with skin they took from me. My voice is talking over my thoughts.

He felt two fingers pulling back his mouth. The glow wasn't from an object in his hand.

As if they were counting his spinal column,

they came into Barney's room with his teeth.

This guy flagging him down, like swinging

a lantern, then he didn't remember.

Barney might have certain anxieties on a trip away

from home because of his racial sensitivities.

He felt something touch the base of his spine,

a finger pushing. Because she never dreamed

of UFOs before. He felt two fingers pulling back

his mouth. As if counting his spinal column.

A red glow in the highway—someone flagging

him down. The glow wasn't from an object

in his hand. *Certain fears might be exaggerated under*

these conditions, making Barney excessively sensitive.

Betty lying on the couch. He was in Philadelphia.

She said, "Call me, Barney." Some of the things

she recounted from dreams he was in: Barney's

teeth taken out, a needle in her navel.

Probably manicure scissors or something,

the being cut off a piece of Betty's fingernail.

Swinging a lantern as if he had one in his hand.

Still sore from where they pulled.

Barney planned to call her anyway. She told them

inside the ship that she would not forget.

Still sore from where they pulled out that needle.

"You must have read my thoughts, Barney,"

she'd say. "I was lying here hoping you would call."

Always so much more in what he's told me than what's in

the dream. Bored, watching her professor

from the front row, sometimes she would think,

"Itch your face, itch your leg." And she

waited to see how long it took him to scratch.

Extraordinary events demand extraordinary proof:

it could be, all the extra he remembers with me

is just part of a dream he didn't remember?

Barney planned to call her anyway. *How can you*

account for "men" who seemed to speak our language

but didn't know things like dentures or aging?

"Itch your face, itch your leg." If they decide

to come back they'll find you, all right.

To see how much power was in thoughts,

all the pain goes away. Something scratched,

lightly, like a stick, against Barney's left arm.

His insistence the visions were his own, making

Barney excessively sensitive.

They were all dressed alike. Betty wasn't really prepared for their appearance.

Tracked by still light,
the slow burning me—

you hover, a halo
struck like chalk
over the operating table.

Your eyes blackening, soupy
and lucid. Nostril slits—
two clove bulbs hovering
over the mouth. Pianist fingers

and needlessly gray. The sterile
pressure of white smoke and ash

around my ribs. You become
undone, the crooked red lifelines
on the bottoms of my feet—

too many of you, cracking
the nave of my arches.
Least thing of my feet, and you

can't take your hands off them.
Star travelers have a lot to learn,

stretching my heels between
their fingers, cherishing them.
Tones struck in the swarm
of those fingers.

She felt very stupid because she didn't know where earth was on the map.

Betty Hill draws the star map they showed her on the ship

Voices slip in salt water, dissolve, the big answer
posing as a secret. The wife in this story is promised

a book to prove what happened. Got a star map instead.

The heavy lines were trade routes and the pilot
said the broken lines were expeditions.

It's unbelievable when her husband points with his eyes closed.

It's something clandestine. They all wore
the same clothes, not quite like men,

not from around here. Is there
a resemblance to the sky which is admitted

to be there and the stars which can be seen. Is there.

Gaudy orange ball, glowing—

> "Later they recall this as what they felt was the huge
> moon that appeared to them to be on the ground."

Maybe it was the fear of remembering it, too.

He still believed what he was seeing had a rational explanation.

Under hypnosis, Barney Hill begins to remember what happened in the White Mountains

A military helicopter having some fun with them.

Jet aircraft flying a low-level mission.

A falling star falling up.

Just an airliner on its way to Montreal.

> What could possibly happen
> at midnight on a deserted
> road in September, the sugar
> maples ready to turn,
> to light up—the woods
> so delicate like a corsage.
>
> Betty's dreams two weeks
> later, six straight nights.
> Seems like an accident
> on the side of the road.
> Barney slows down each time.
>
> Always three of them, thick-
> chested, slender-hipped
> approaching Barney's door.
>
> They take him from the car.
> Five coming to Betty's side.
>
> She tries to open her door.
> They do it for her.

The round object shifted position from right to left in front of the car, hovered again in mid-air.

It wasn't a satellite. It saw them and changed course and flung itself around the mountain—an impossible curve—to investigate them.

Keep coming closer, the voice said. Keep the binoculars to your eyes and you won't be harmed.

Fifty miles south of the Colebrook restaurant where customers in booths at the window watched them get out of the car. White people groping with their eyes— *what's she doing with a Negro?*

A row of curved windows uptilted like a raised eyebrow. Cold blue-white fluorescent glow, red light on either side.

It was no longer spinning.

> *I think the whole*
> *experience was so*
> *improbable and*
> *fantastic to the witness—*
> *along with the very*
> *real fear of being*
> *captured added*
> *to imagined fears—*
> *that his mind*
> *refused to believe*
> *what his eyes*
> *were perceiving*
> *and a mental*
> *block resulted.*

Daniel Webster Highway, an almost uninhabitable region.

Through the window, 11 figures, human form, pulling levers. The cold precision of German officers. Leader in glossy leather, a scarf draped over his left shoulder.

> Code-like beeping, back
> of the car—they could feel it
> vibrate every beep when
> they drove away.
>
> Delsey under the front seat
> the whole time, sitting still,
> tight as a ball. The dog shook
> in her sleep, kicked her legs
> as if running, even weeks after
> they got home (and the strange
> fungus, was it a mistake
> not to bathe her right away).
>
> The ease with which this craft
> seemed to move and stop,
> and the absolute lack of any
> sound at this close range.

The pressure of their arms. Small men holding him, suspended. Dragging him, scraping the tops of his shoes.

This is something that really serves no purpose. Great harm can come if you don't forget.

Dr. Simon put Barney Hill under hypnosis. Barney described the humanoids. David Baker drew them.

Gas-fogged cat eyes clamped
over mine. He never blinked.

A swampy glow wrapped around
each side of the creature's face.

You'd have to run your finger
from front to back of the head

just to trace his cheek bones.
So ordinary, so round, a head

cavity large enough to contain
those eyeballs, hold a brain

our size. A ferocious mumbling,
a membrane over the mouth, maybe

sheathing the body of the entity.

Wide cheeked, weak chinned.
The plume of those eyes—

if there's a membrane, it kept out
irritants and he didn't need to blink

to lubricate his autocratic orbs.
No spoken words, only grunts,

prowling hums. Mouth a slit
knifed into wood. A dusty

blue light radiated from the walls—
I could've been soaking in a tub

of water. They might be any color
but didn't seem to have faces

different from white men.
He sucked air into piggish

nostrils, rocking back his head.
I saw no bone or nose cartilage.

No hair. No ears, just holes.
A sea wind made me shudder.

He was told not to open his eyes and it would be over
quickly and he could be on his way.

I felt my shoes removed, my pants opened.
The examination table too small for my height
or anyone's. My feet dangled off the bottom.
The frightening part was the military precision.
The floors were smooth, the room pale blue—
no, sky-blue. I didn't hear footsteps when they
walked us to our examination rooms.

*   *   *

This is what stargazers see through gigantic telescopes
and they don't even know. The room so clean,
I closed my eyes. They turned me over. It was about
the size of a cigar, like a tube, larger than a pencil,
and it went in easily. Then was withdrawn.
Something they'd throw away after getting
what they wanted. I remembered putting my gun
in the car in case of bears and the hostility of white people
when they see Betty and me. I felt no pain but it hurt
to be in this room. They take us out of our cars.
They know where to find us.

*   *   *

The examiner said I wouldn't remember anything
because it wasn't painful and I wanted to forget.
And it helped, telling me what I wanted.

*   *   *

I had an ear infection when I was a little boy—
Dr. Harley wanted to stick one of those
scopes in it. He said you peep inside the body,

light it up. I'm on my stomach, their doctor
pushing something inside me and it feels like
what I think went in my ear.

*   *   *

I will be very careful. I will cooperate and won't
be harmed. They pulled it back out of me—
came out easily—and counted my spinal column.
All of this occurred and I didn't know it was true.
I sat on my gun when they brought me back to our car.

Transcript: Barney Hill's Hypnosis

He fell deeper and deeper, deeper asleep.
Drew circles in the air, called them eyes.
Fully relaxed, deeper and deeper asleep,
he traced a curve for the left cheek

and stuck another eye on it.
An afterthought, he gave it a scarf,
traced two curves into a cap and visor.
Barney's head nodded into his chest.

He gave it a scarf and the doctor said,
"You are fully relaxed, no fear, no anxiety."
Head nodding, his chest exposed,
thought he saw a plane going to Montreal—

fully relaxed, no fear, anxiety—
he heard a fly buzzing, about to land,
thought he saw a plane but it hovered.
A row of lights, tilting, leveled off.

He felt like a fly buzzing against a screen.
Their eyes: Barney froze in the grass
as a row of lights, tilting, leveled off.
Strange faces at the window looking down—

their eyes, Barney froze in the grass.
A pilot, in shiny black coat, visor,
ordered the faces away from the window.
You will not be troubled by what you remember.

The pilot's shiny black coat, visor
terrified Barney, so he hustled to the car
(*Your memories won't trouble you—I am here—*)
and Betty pleading drive, drive, don't look back.

Terrified, Barney hustled the car into gear.
A few miles later, a bright streak along the road,
Betty pleading go back, back, turn back around.

Barney grabbed the tire wrench below his seat.

A bright streak lit up the midnight road,
three of them on the highway stopped the car.
Barney afraid the wrench would seem a weapon.
They won't trouble you here. Your sleep is deeper.

Three of them on the highway stopped the car
then helped him out of the driver's seat.
They won't trouble you here. Your sleep is deeper.
Eyes closed; felt his feet drag

as they guided him up a smooth incline,
fully relaxed, deeper and deeper asleep—
he didn't want to be operated on—
deeper and deeper, he fell deeper asleep.

The Orb

I say anytime you see a light in the sky, check it out.
                                        —Betty Hill

I'm not ashamed to say I wanted a sighting.
I drove north into the White Mountains
for research. Nothing bookish: the kind
where an orange light grows plump, pulsates,
follows me down a deserted wilderness road.
I'm on the lookout for stories with more
complications, witnesses, three lacquered
disks in formation, or maybe they looked
like porcelain in starlight, their impossible
evasive gymnastics when a passenger jet
heads their way. I wanted to do a double-take—
a cigar shape drifting in front of the moon.

                    *   *   *

I imagine first contact to be like the time
I saw a deer running from police on my
overpopulated street in Chicago: a creature
so formidable you want to freeze the moment,
study every flickering pigment. Lucky for me
this deer who could've cracked open an SUV
between its haunches was running on the other
side of the street, too scared to know
I was watching. A perfect alien encounter.

                    *   *   *

More rain. On the third day a slant
of light, visions of October leafage
swabbed in outlandish color—my favorite,
the brute, plum-tomato reds gushing
on the maples across the street from
my hotel like washes of electric guitar.

                    *   *   *

The day I tried another drive to the Hills'
abduction site, Felix Baumgartner bunny-
hopped out of a balloon sponsored by
an energy-drink company and flew through
the stratosphere above Roswell, New Mexico.
Edward Archbold died after winning
a cockroach-eating contest in Miami.

*   *   *

Chased back again by rain and fog on twisty
roads in the White Mountains. A few miles
from Durham, on Route 108, during a clearing
lull in the rainstorm, I saw a bright dollop
of light in the sky, a white orb, and nearly
drove myself off the road (now I know why
Barney Hill pulled their car into a picnic area).
Probably a helicopter, even though I saw
no tail outline or taillight. In my rearview
mirror, I glimpsed the ditch I could've crashed
into—and I lost my nerve. Kept driving.

*   *   *

Betty never questioned *her* nerve.
She chided her captors for performing
medical tests on her nerves—such nerve,
she said, kidnapping people right off
the highway. Her first sighting,
mid-1950s: the craft exploded in midair,
the Air Force explained it was a meteor.
She collected heavy fragments of wreckage
but couldn't find anyone willing
to analyze their chemical composition.
Three weeks before her abduction,
she scattered the pieces in her backyard
during a gravel delivery. They're buried
where the stones are spread.

Ask the Bibliomancy Oracle

*With thanks to Regie Cabico, Oliver de la Paz, Frank O'Hara, Rebecca Loudon,
and James Longenbach*

Reb Livingston invites me to like
the Bibliomancy Oracle on Facebook.
OK, but first a few questions.

Were Barney and Betty Hill
captured by aliens from
the Zeta Reticuli star system?

> *The voice on the machine isn't you
> even though it says it is.*

Was the star map they showed
Betty in the spacecraft real?

> *In the labyrinth, there is constantly
> the problem of proximity. How
> what is understood about where
> you stand depends on where you stand.*

Did the aliens' medical
experiments leave 21 warts
in a perfect circle on Barney?

> *It is easy to be beautiful;
> it is difficult to appear so.*

Did their hypnosis sessions
with Dr. Simon reveal repressed
memories of the abduction?

> *I don't know how to do it.
> I stand on my hind legs and bark.
> I want more. I want more. I want more.*

Is the stain on Betty's dress extraterrestrial?

> *Today, no matter if it rains,
> It's time to follow the path into the forest.*

Extraordinary claims require extraordinary evidence.

He was easy
to love, Betty

said, and was
loved. It's

that simple
and even

people who
didn't know

him can say this.
We didn't

bathe Delsey
those first

few days after
our capture

and we
watched

her die.
The rank stains

where they
touched

my dress,
blue light

coming from
the walls

in the exam-
ination room:

whatever
they shoved

inside
Barney, we

couldn't
even tell

our closest
friends.

The problem is to see what the sky would look like from their home base.

Betty Hill receives a letter from Marjorie Fish, amateur astronomer

1.

Dear Betty, I hope you don't mind
I'm using your first name. I feel
I know you. They always say it,
afraid I'm a killjoy, when, really,
the damage is done. Nothing could be
more isolating than what I've seen.
We have a lot in common.
They rammed a scroll in a language
no one understands down my
throat, and when I spit it back
everyone's embarrassed, like I'm
forcing them to witness a live birth
or watch a fish eat its own eggs.
We were chased by the nighttime sky.
My main love is anthropology, so I am
quite concerned and sympathetic with
the Negro cause. In the basement
four months ago, snowed-in with
the rest of the state, playing pool,
a blue-green flash stung Barney
in back of the neck and he fell
up the stairs—fell forward,
could not stand, tried to creep
the rest of the way and I called
an ambulance and he was gone.
I'm getting carried away. My loneliness
hangs upside-down in a cave.

2.

I've been working on the star map
you drew four years now and several
patterns like your map turned up.

35

I'm getting closer to solving the mystery.
A random letter from a stranger
is an incident. A sign you're forced
to leave one room and enter another.
And this room is a necessary torching:
stars that could support planets
with life are not scattered at random.
The problem is to see what the sky
would look like from their home base.
She's making a 3-D model,
looking for my map in the actual stars.
She's asking questions, stringing beads
on nylon fishing wire and calling it
the universe—this is the proof
Barney always wanted, not a ring
of warts they left behind or my
choking when I remember
where they stuck me with the needle
no one wants to believe anyway.
A chariot in the sky, its rims
full of eyes—go ask Ezekiel if
vision made him a wallflower.
Did the map look like a drawing
or a photograph? Were the stars
in color, or white on a black
background, or black on white?
A tiny spider rappelling from
the ceiling for no good reason—
this is proof something happened.

Beeping sounds in isolated locations all over the world, driving away animals.

Any psychic abilities I might have had were gone, never to return.
—Betty Hill

Someone heard a steady beep-beep-beep, regular intervals, weeks at a time.

They moved through you like tinnitus then disappeared when you stepped away.

An astronomer in Keene endured a torrent, 16 hours straight, followed by eight hours of silence.

I relieved my boredom that year chewing gum, whispering and talking in class, pinching students and wearing a green garden snake around my wrist as a bracelet.

I learned to spot flares in the smallest places.

Mother knew I was reading a book about faeries. Look for them early in the day, she said, in the garden, while you can still see dew on the flowers.

Then she thought if they're so smart, let them find Barney's grave without her help.

A week after the funeral, driving along Rt. 125.
Two red lights floating each side of a telephone pole.
They cut across the highway as Betty got closer,
stopped in front of her. She pulled over.
A double row of windows, shadows in dim light.
The disc hovering, the silence almost belligerent.

It was like what captured them eight years ago:
she looked for the Nazi, his black scarf, the Examiner.
What moved in the windows were silhouettes.
One of the shadows limped, like it had a broken
ankle, but that's also how the beings breathed (gimpy).

She remembered blue-sky light radiating from
the walls and a map unrolled from a slot in a wall—
three-dimensional holes pocked all over the universe.
Some map lines for their trade routes, some for expeditions.
It was her story now. She opened both car doors—

they could see no one was with her. Do you want
to know where Barney is, she thought. Barney died.
He's no longer alive. It hovered. She was crying
now and slammed the passenger door shut.
Everything was moving so fast she couldn't

even see it blur. Everything ordinary, that is.
She felt like she did eight years ago, knew
they could read her thoughts. The ship
tilted like a plate balanced atop a juggler's stick:
how does it stay perched, you think, and it's not

supposed to look so graceful. She pointed
to the cemetery two miles away and thought
about how they could find him by the flowers
on his plot. It rocked back and forth three times
then crossed the highway toward the graveyard.

"Over time other miracles occurred, but these were the most important ones."

It's ordinary to load up the car
and spend the weekend somewhere
else—two ordinary people love
each other the most ordinary ways,

one of them making sandwiches for
the drive, the other packing suitcases.
It wasn't this way in the war, everyone
on guard for invasions from the sky,

you couldn't drive at night: no outdoor
lamps, your headlights taped. Nothing
but a meager beam would show if Japanese
planes flew over looking for targets.

Betty remembers an electrician standing
on the kitchen table, installing her family's
first light. The glow floated like a balloon
until it spread everywhere. And a radio

built by her grandfather covered a whole
dining room wall. A scientist came over
the wireless, saying if a car could travel
60 mph, gravity would crush the passengers.

If everyone was quiet and she pressed his
headphones to her ears, voices came out
of the wall (if there wasn't too much static).
Neighbors sat with them, hoping to hear

a voice (usually faint), so much fuzz you
really couldn't understand what was said.
People didn't put up the black veil if
you talked about seeing things, back then.

Her living room should have been a cave with a candle and fire hearth.

Libraries shouldn't be so emotional:
I sat with my laptop at a long, oak table

in the University of New Hampshire
archives, the Betty and Barney Hill Papers,

reading Betty's journal entry from
the day Barney was killed by a stroke:

after a game of pool in their basement,
the entire state shut down by a monster

February blizzard and Barney winning
every game, joking he could beat her with

one hand tied behind his back,
he felt a sting, like a hornet's,

in back of his neck and he collapsed:
ambulance delayed by unplowed roads,

he slipped into a coma less than
a half hour after finally making it

to the emergency room, the doctor telling
Betty it's hopeless, just pray he dies quickly,

and that night, she wrote in her journal:
"I sat, wrapped in a blanket—I thought

it should have been a bearskin, my
living room should have been a cave

with a candle and fire hearth, while I
waited for 46-year-old Barney to die":

I looked around the archive, the Head
of Special Collections talking on the phone

about the library's Robert Frost Papers,
and three tables behind me a journalist

researched the Hills for a *Skeptical Inquirer*
article, taking digital photos of Betty's

correspondence (later, I turned down
her request to create a "Betty Hill Poetry

Contest"): I don't think I've ever felt
such physical loss in the quiet, walled-off

vault of a library reading room,
taking notes from Betty's words on

a yellowing page composed 40 years
ago (the electric typewriter's cursive

font, her preferred typeface for nearly
everything she wrote): I could hear

in Betty's voice a grieving monotone,
eviscerated, the same exhausted

pitch I remember from my father
describing my mother's stroke in 1999:

she wrote a check to Mellon Bank for
their monthly car payment, she was

watching a *Matlock* repeat and he heard
a moan—an animal keening—and found her

moving her mouth up and down,
body shrunk into itself, heaving,

no sound, eyes astonished and terrified,
blood crossing into her brain, destroying it.

Elegy for Barney Hill

Barney slapped
his neck

and said
a hornet

stung him.
He wanted to

sit down.
There are no

hornets in a February
snowstorm.

Sightings Journal

A swarm of lights bouncing around like tennis balls in front of Betty Hill's car— *some deep purple,* she writes in her diary, the color of spots that cluster before your eyes right before you faint.

Betty marked her wedding (June 28) and abduction (Sept. 19) anniversaries every year in the journal.

She started it almost a decade after her husband, Barney, died. Handwritten in three spiral notebooks, retyped as a single manuscript.

A dead man takes flight in the white space and comes back in beams, flashes, beeping sounds, disappearing cars, and the 22 times Betty heard train sounds from empty tracks.

She called the diary, "Sightings Journal." Her kidnappers and their interstellar kin come off as civilized, which makes them even scarier.

As Barney rises from the page, so does my father. Betty's deep purple blots dissolve, I wake my father in the nursing home's recreation room—final time I saw him—dark except for the DVD of *Con Air* playing on the television cart between the 100-gallon fish tank and card table.

"It's not about UFOs," Liz said after she read my photocopy of the journal. "It's Betty missing Barney."

I know what it's like to think you can write the dead back to life as if you have any say in the matter.

I'm still angry I remember Nicolas Cage's mullet just as clearly as the light from the flat-screen TV that ruffled my dad's burgundy track suit.

The light hurt my eyes—wind snapping an awning. Last time I saw any kind of glow from my father's living body.

Shrill gun battles, an explosion receding behind us (Nicolas Cage couldn't do anything to stop the convicts from taking over the plane) as I wheeled him into the hallway, same wing my mother died in. I noticed fugitive spots of spilled food spattered all over his collar and chest.

Told him I met someone named Liz. He said, out of nowhere, maybe we'd get married one day. Either prescient or a lucky guess.

Torn right from the bone, the dead disappear into thin air to become luminous objects in the sky we write about.

Barney Hill ascends in the journal like Keats in Shelley's *Adonais*, one more planet kindling the universe.

Betty stands at the edge of the railroad tracks, watching the stars.

She logged 2,998 UFO sightings, 204 trips to the tracks in Exeter, between 1983 and 1989.

"Actual count," she writes on the journal's first page, "less than those actually seen."

I tried not to use the past tense when we spoke. I didn't want him to feel like everything was already over.

The crossword lately made him dizzy.

We didn't talk much. I had to leave an hour later to catch a plane back to Chicago.

My god, how we wreck ourselves keeping the dead alive.

It disappeared behind a mailbox on Dunlapsville Road.

Dear Mrs. Hill,
in the end
remember
I told you so.
Please have
a very Merry
Christmas and
joyous New Year.

Dear Betty,
first thing
they said
was, "Don't
be alarmed.
We've talked
to people
before."

Dear Mrs. Hill, the larger one
swallowed the smaller through the beam,
a tiny dot in the glow before they merged.
The weather was rainy.

Dear Betty, It made no sound when we
stopped to get a picture. Not even
crickets.

Dear ~~Mr. Bjork,~~ Mrs. Hill,

Like most Americans you have been supremely disinformed. The ETs use humans for food on a regular basis with the concurrence of the American government. In return for the human food, we receive alien technology.

Dear Betty,
they admitted
not knowing
anything about
farming—
claimed they
lived off
the atmosphere
like it was
hamburgers.
We couldn't
survive
a year in outer
space, they said,
and we're silly
for even trying.

Dear Betty, I would
like you to tell me
the aliens are cute
after they have cut out
your rectum while you
are still alive.
It is uncomfortable
and most humans
do not survive this ordeal.

Dear Betty, I was given a bar with symbols
molded into it and which is under analysis.

Dear Mrs. Hill,

Enclosed is a book which will enlighten you in
regard to Spiritualism, and which, we hope, will
cause you to have nothing to do with the "Prince
of the Power of the Air" (the title the Bible gives
to the Devil).

Dear Mrs. Hill, my husband, Gary, was spreading manure.
They asked him for fertilizer. *You'll have to walk with me
to the barn,* he said. They changed the subject. The afternoon
they disappeared, he laid a new bag of peat moss on top
a load of manure. Drove up the hill, dumped it where
the spaceships had been sitting. Next morning it was gone.

Dear Betty,
my friend
Janet Waverly
and I believe
in UFOs—
not in a scientific
or technical way,
but theologically.
We know,
as you do,
that they exist
and we must
try to see this
in relation to
Christ's redemption.

Dear Mrs. Hill, I realize that big-headed,
slant-eyed extraterrestrials want at least
two half-African-American people, or else
why would they put a needle in your navel
and then turn around and take samples from
Barney's groin? Was that to get some sperm?
I think so.

Dear Mrs. Hill, Please understand I'm not trying to persuade you to get involved in my case. If you don't want to, I'll understand. I'm making a concentrated effort to confirm my case and the incidents. The facts, bizarre as they are, surrounding my abduction—I'm sure if you called Wendell, he'd Xerox-copy everything.

Dear Betty—Could you give me some recent examples of encounters you've had with UFOs that might help illustrate how "mischievous" they can be and, more seriously, how cruel or dangerous they can be? This is very important since the average public person thinks he or she could just walk up to a landed craft and say hello.

If She Only Had Proof Something Happened

Stranger in gray suit—neighbor's dog went berserk behind glass door. Left huge footprints without any heel marks. Police were called. Betty saw the ship glide over crossing signals, blue light above the tracks too far away to film.

She wanted to explain to someone her eyes wouldn't focus. She dropped a quarter and was too dizzy to bend over.

Squad cars came. A false alarm, they said. She remembered the kidnappers passing Barney's false teeth back and forth: everything she believed held at arm's length like bloody gristle from bone.

She knew they left soot in the trees, fire in the flower gardens.

The two witnesses prophesied for 1,260 days wearing sackcloths.

Dear Mr. and Mrs. Hill—We have read about your experience with the Flying Saucer and the beings who operated it. We are thoroughly convinced that you had contact with fallen angels who were once in heaven but who were cast out along with their leader, Satan.

Mary's body is not hidden somewhere.
Even if you had proper cameras, you couldn't see her.

What are Mary's molecules doing—the atoms in her body, you know.
Her body has been glorified now.

Jesus's and Mary's bodies are in Heaven. His body was ascended, Mary's
    assumed.
But now their physical bodies take up spaces.

Remember, Jesus has been able to go through doors and walls.
He was able to appear and disappear.

Heaven is beyond our experience right now, like it's another dimension.
The only way to reach Heaven is you die, then God allows you to go.

A woman clothed with the sun, a woman with the moon under her feet.
A woman with a crown of 12 stars on her head.

The woman about to give birth.
But Mary's already had that child.

Very Few Were Like Planes

On my way home, I saw nothing. But I wished them happy holidays. Thanked them for the weather.

Four rows of white lights. Didn't have time to count them all. Fog appeared around the craft.

Parked my car at the curve. I saw one of them near the road.

A quiet night. Then wind blowing. Car rocking back and forth, but the trees not moving.

One set of keys separated from my ring and my watch stopped.

A policeman told me six reports. Craft seen along Rt. 286, Seabrook.

I flashed my lights again. The craft went dark. *If you can hear and understand me,* I asked, *put your lights back on.* Nothing. *If you know me, put your lights on.*

Lost my nerve and did not repeat my message. Drove toward the tracks. Stopped to thank them for our weather.

At Pic N Pay deli counter, clerk told me she and her husband watched a UFO at 4 a.m. on January 25 in the direction of Eliot. She lives in York. Also told me a friend of hers saw a big cigar-shaped one flying around the shipyard about a year ago.

I went out with Stephen and his friend Pam from NYC. While they were here, Pres. Reagan was shot.

We left Portsmouth about 7:30. Saw a cluster of blue flashes and one briefly over the tracks.

I heard a rooster crowing. None in the area to my knowledge.

*   *   *   *   *

Over the tracks—not the same kind of disk I've seen for years. But like the one I filmed in front of my house. One light on each side. Dull, dark metal object.

Portsmouth Police came. They said I'd called to report a prowler around my home. Not true.

I drove to the tracks, stopped, gave my signal. Loud rooster crowings, a constant sound.

Usually Thursday nights very busy and Tuesdays quiet. Reversal this week.

22nd anniversary of our capture. I went out alone. Very few were like planes. At the bridge, one was flying over the tracks low, below the treetops, using one single red light. It stopped. So did I.

No prowler and no marks in the snow.

* * * * *

A Russian satellite picked up a distress signal beeper. Reports of two planes colliding in Stratham over Great Bay.

Clerk at the Bread Box told me her brother and wife saw a UFO in Amesbury two weeks ago, about 8:30 p.m. Same circular shape, lighted windows, small lights on the craft—just like the one that captured us.

Their son came home, scared. The brother called Pease Air Force Base, who wanted him to come in, make a report. He refused.

A warm night. Moon half-full, clear.

I wanted to see if they would come in the same pattern.

* * * * *

Mystery solved: a private plane in Stratham had been broken into and robbed. Beeper thrown to the ground and was going off.

* * * * *

I drove and the craft rose up, treetop level, as if watching me.

I greeted it and said tonight was our 22nd anniversary—that I was the lone survivor of "the interrupted journey." It came closer, over the field.

When I picked up my binoculars, it went dark. I explained the binoculars and said they were safe, but it stayed unlit.

Oct. 23, 1975: Tom Snyder Interviews
Betty Hill on *The Tomorrow Show*

TV producers wanted an all-black
or all-white couple to play
the Hills' parts. Betty held out
until 1975, when Universal
decided to cast black actor
James Earl Jones as Barney,
and Estelle Parsons, who's white,
to play Betty. It was the year
of the most famous World Series
in history, and Betty's Red Sox
won Game 6—the one baseball
historians call an epic, which
in their lingo really does mean
a long poem, a tale of the tribe—
and I stayed up until 12:30, riveted
by my idol, portly cigar-puffing
Red Sox pitcher Luis Tiant,
"El Tiante," Cuban exile.
My family approved: in their
immigrant anxiety, comparing
the number of white players to black,
Tiant, as a Cuban, was not really
black, didn't count in the tabulation.
No one allowed for the possibility
that Sicilians were dark as El Tiante.
I could wager my stupid, ballplayer-
idolizing heart on his tired arm
and walrus mustache and, for
a change, my brother wouldn't
punch me for being a race traitor.

The producers flew Betty
to New York—a private
screening and an appearance
on Tom Snyder's *Tomorrow Show*
the night of Game 7. "I daresay,"
Snyder dared to say, buzzing
with hyperbole, as always,
a cigarette between his fingers,
as always, "if anybody had gone

to an EKG machine after the Boston
and Cincinnati game last night,
there might've been a few peaks
and valleys in the electro-
cardiogram report" (actually,
most fans in the Eastern Time Zone,
like me, went straight to bed
after Game 6). Tom asked how
neighbors treated them afterward:
"Did people think ol' Betty and
ol' Barney had just, you know,
gone over the hill? That the pilot
light is gone?" NBC played
Paul McCartney and Wings,
"Venus and Mars are all right
tonight," before each commercial
segment, a song I listened to
(my portable cassette player, which
I carried around like the teddy
bear I'd outgrown) while doing
spelling homework. "The problem is
the little stories that get in the way,"
Tom said, "like the fellow
in Wisconsin who had 14 million
little men and women in bushel
baskets in his basement who were
going to take him and his wife
away after Christmas until
the end of the world. You have to
sift out all the ding-a-lings
and bushel baskets in basements."
Someone in Portsmouth painted
a swastika on their sidewalk,
splattered their car with eggs.
The aliens, she said, were not
color-blind television executives.
Abduction itself isn't good
enough for them. Sometimes
they're forced to cast interracial
couples in made-for-TV movies.

From Outer Space with Love

One couple tuned in for two hours.
The voice, sexless, returned, one-third

the size of the moon, a typewriter
moving across the sky. Television sets

quite by accident picked it up and phoned
electromagnetic insults to the nervous

system. A radio talking in their image
to probe their bodies. New frequencies

broadcasting all over their muddled
little planet. A loud hum.

Several nights later, they made a list
of questions. Who sees you

in more planets than Earth?
Whose intentions take physical form?

> *You refuse to trespass upon your garden.*
> *You are both of little value.*

A voice box slow-moving in the mountains.

Two little ones traversing the night sky,
tilted upward in panic.

The UFO Incident (Directed by Richard A. Colla, 1975)

The following story is based on actual transcripts of the reel-to-reel tapes
made by Betty (Estelle Parsons) and Barney (James Earl Jones) under hypnosis
by Dr. Simon (Barnard Hughes, the veteran character actor who played
a nervous con man named Jack Spicer in a 1971 episode of the television series
Cannon—not that Jack Spicer, of course, the poet who claimed that writing
was the equivalent of dictated radio transmissions received from Martians).

Autumn sunset, the White Mountains, sky rash-red like a photo of the Martian
horizon—so begins our captivity narrative. All the action will occur on tape,
recovered memories unspooling in Dr. Simon's office. For the teleplay writers,
the great challenge, it seems, was to make Betty and Barney Hill's hypnotherapy
sessions terrifying to viewers accustomed to paint-by-number 1970s police series
procedurals. Studio execs were nervous about casting interracial actors to play

the Hills, but, all the same, green-lighted the aliens' blue skin. C-list actors play
blue astronauts the Hills claimed were gray. Our spacemen first appear marching
out of the dark New England wood with the creepy, anthropological seriousness
of zookeepers. After several cuts between close-ups of Dr. Simon's rolling tape
machine and these creatures sheathed in blue latex—I'd have to be hypnotized
to believe their body-stockings were actually skin—I decided I couldn't write

this poem without looking up who wore the alien suits. So where does a writer
go for sestina research? Wikipedia and IMDB, natch. The actor who played
"The Leader," Lou Wagner, first made a name for himself uttering the mesmerizing
words of the chimp Lucius—"You can't trust the older generation!"—in *Planet
of the Apes* (a precocious teen, he was Zira's nephew), before Taylor went traipsing
down the beach with his mute galpal, Nova, their horse performing a series

of alternating trots and gallops before stumbling upon that film's most serious
and arresting image: Lady Liberty, buried to her shoulders in the sand, written
off as an ancient, apocalyptic ruin. The Leader is the alien on Dr. Simon's tapes
Barney feared most. No longer the charming Lucius, now Wagner played
The Leader like the brute Nazi Barney felt he was—not some little green Martian.
These latexed, cat-eyed Zeta Reticulans were rapists. It took hypnotherapy

to reveal the Hills' repressed sexual trauma. That is, if you believe hypnosis
recovers actual memories (Simon was skeptical). What could be more serious
and alienating (whether the Hills actually were probed by Zeta Reticulans
or it was a fraud invented by a couple who should've been writing

sci-fi) than to have your assault dismissed by skeptics who claim you're playing
a hoax? Would the publicity-shy Hills fake an attack, then document it on tape

during hypnosis? Not that these questions actually emerge from the script
or any kind of serious cinematography. After all, this is a film that chose to play
aliens in fetish outfits and waste footage on countless close-ups of reel-to-reel tapes.

—For Jeffery Conway

Betty Hill, "Sightings Journal": April 28, 1978

Late, a cold night (for April
   anyway), parked near the railroad
   crossing. She couldn't see much
but tracks tapering off the horizon,
           two map lines

swinging toward a bare point so far
   away it vanished when she
   blinked. Turned the motor off.
Lights of the Mothership, flickering—
           size of a nickel if you

held your thumb to the sky—
   appeared over traffic on Rt. 125.
   And then she heard a happy
family picnic, children laughing,
           other people talking

about the food. She couldn't
   swear to it, but it sounded
   just like the picnic last summer
at her mother's home.
           And knew not to tell anyone.

September 19, 1961, An Index

BEAMS, FLASHES

1978: Apr. 15, Apr. 18, May 30 (searchlights); 1979: Feb. 20 (a "cone" of light came up to the tops of the trees), Jun. 1 (a beam shaped like a cylinder, with straight sides and square at the top), Aug. 13 (many beams, varying in size from small to large with several craft flying toward them), Sept. 14 (many small balls of light bouncing around and in front of her car—some deep purple in color), Nov. 6 (beam from bottom of a craft going to the signal box); 1980: Jan. 15 (saw one put down a white beam toward the ground), Apr. 10 (round, red flash seen in front seat of her car; the next day—facial sunburn), May 25 (tree lighted twice from white flashes), Jun. 7 (four beams), Aug. 14 (searchlights and flashes, some over her car), Sept. 9 (flashing lights)

BEEPING SOUNDS HEARD

1978: Apr. 28 (2 a.m., in her backyard); 1979: Oct. 23 (at the crossing); 1980: Apr. 1 (daylight on Route 108), Apr. 18 (at the crossing); 1981: Jun 28 (at the crossing); 1983: Feb 28 (heard for five minutes, at the crossing), Oct. 5 (at the crossing)

CHURCH BELLS—NO SOURCE

1987: May 9, May 16 (South Hampton Road at 10:00 p.m.); 1989: May 5, May 22, Aug. 10 (rang nine times), Sept. 4 (rang six times), Nov. 18 (rang three times)

DISAPPEARING CARS (SEEN, HEARD, AND DISAPPEARED)

1977: Aug. 25, Sept. 19; 1978: Apr. 6, Apr. 23, Aug. 23, Nov 9; 1979: Feb. 9, Feb. 11, Apr. 22, Jul. 13 (Rangeley, Maine); 1980: Aug. 13, Aug. 16 (Route 101, Stratham), Oct. 22; 1981: Jan. 25, Mar. 16, Nov. 5; 1982: Apr. 29

SOUNDS OF A TRAIN BUT NO TRAIN

1979: Dec. 8 (sounds of a train under a bridge), Jul. 8 (a triangle-shaped craft making the sounds of a train); 1980: Jun. 3, Dec. 9 (heard for 15 minutes); 1981: Mar 15; 1982: Apr. 29, May 19, Oct. 24, Dec. 1, Dec. 17; 1984: Dec. 20; 1985: Jan. 10, Jan. 16, Mar. 18, July 18, Oct. 26; 1986: Apr. 20; 1987: May 16; 1988: Dec. 12; 1989: Feb. 19, Feb. 26, Aug. 10-11

Notes

"'Now do you believe in flying saucers?'"

> Title taken from Betty Hill's words to Barney Hill after returning to their car, September 19, 1961. According to Walter Webb's October 26, 1961, report for the National Investigations Committee on Aerial Phenomena (NICAP), Betty asked this question near Ashland, New Hampshire, 35 miles south of the alleged abduction site.

"'My soul sometimes floats out of my body. I don't listen to the radio while driving.'"

> Collages material from Barney Hill's hypnosis transcripts and Michael A. Persinger, "The UFO Experience: A Normal Correlate of Human Brain Function."

"'What I'm saying is part of me outside the actual creation of words themselves.'"

> Hypnosis tape playback, April 5, 1964.

"He felt two fingers pulling back his mouth. The glow wasn't from an object in his hand."

> Italics adapted from John G. Fuller, The Interrupted Journey.

"She felt very stupid because she didn't know where earth was on the map."

> Adapts a line from Gertrude Stein, "Rooms." Quotation from Fuller, *The Interrupted Journey.*

"He still believed what he was seeing had a rational explanation."

> Adapts Webb's October 26, 1961, report on the Hill case for NICAP.

"Dr. Simon put Barney Hill under hypnosis. Barney described the humanoids. David Baker drew them."

> "'I can just describe it,' Barney recalls, 'as if it were like getting into a hot tub of water and soaking, as if every nerve in my body would be pleasant and tingling. It was something I had never been able to achieve before. Just a tingling, pleasant glow, just like a rubdown'" (Fuller, *The Interrupted Journey*).

"The Orb"

> Information on Betty Hill's first sighting adapted from her November 13, 1980, letter to Bob Hair.

"Ask the Bibliomancy Oracle":

> Special thanks to Reb Livingston's Bibliomancy Oracle Tumblr. Poems quoted in italics (in order of appearance): Regie Cabico, "The Hudson Wakes You Up Each Morning"; Oliver de la Paz, "Labyrinth 59"; Frank O'Hara, "Meditations in an Emergency"; Rebecca Loudon, "What I didn't say when the gasworks shook their iron tails in my direction"; James Longenbach, "By the Same Author."

"The problem is to see what the sky would look like from their home base."

> Adapts material from Marjorie Fish letter to Betty Hill, June 8, 1969.

"Over time other miracles occurred, but these were the most important ones."

> Adapts material from Betty Hill, "Miracles" (unpublished essay).

"It disappeared behind a mailbox on Dunlapsville Road."

> John H. Reynolds letter to Richard Harris Hall, Acting Director of NICAP, May 23, 1966: "The Hills receive, on the average, a telephone call per day from residents reporting UFOs."

"Very Few Were Like Planes"

> Adapts material from Betty Hill's "Sightings Journal."

Photo by Kevin Nance

Tony Trigilio's recent books include *Ghosts of the Upper Floor* and *Inside the Walls of My Own House*, both from BlazeVOX [books]. His selected poems, *Fuera del Taller del Cosmos*, was published in Guatemala by Editorial Poe (translated by Bony Hernández). He coedits the journal *Court Green* and is an associate editor for *Tupelo Quarterly*. He lives in Chicago.

TITLES FROM MARSH HAWK PRESS

──────────── ARTISTIC ADVISORY BOARD ────────────

For more information, please go to: **www.marshhawkpress.org**